the like of it

the like of it

Poems by:

Karen Annesen

Edward Barker

Katy Evans-Bush

Heather Holden

Simon Rees-Roberts

Liane Strauss

the like of it: *an anthology of poetry*
Copyright : the authors

First published 2005 by Baring & Rogerson Books, the sister
poetry imprint to Sickle Moon Books, part of Eland Publishing
Ltd, 61 Exmouth Market, Clerkenwell, London EC1 4QL.

Designed by Roger Huddle
Typeset in 10/13.5 Adobe Sabon and FF Din.

Printed by Aldgate Press, Units 5&6, Gunthorpe Street
Workshops, 3 Gunthorpe Street, London E1 7RQ

ISBN: 1-903651-04-2

Contact authors: thelikeofit@gmail.com

Acknowledgements

The authors would like to acknowledge the following
publications, in which some of these poems first
appeared: *Magma, The Wolf, The Liberal, Limelight*
(www.thepoem.co.uk), nthposition.com
We would like to thank: Roger Huddle for designing
and typesetting the book; Emil Smith for his creative
and technical help; May Cornet and Roddy Lumsden.

Foreword

Baring and Rogerson are to be commended for bringing these six marvellous poets to a wider public attention. This unusual concept for an anthology works wonderfully. It complements Baring and Rogerson's celebrated *Poetry of Place* series perfectly. There is, in any genuine poetry, a sense of travel and an expectancy of strange, new territories. The various formal dexterities, emotional breadths and intellectual insights of these poets will ensure a thrilling trip.

Whilst Karen Annesen's intelligent and poised poetry, for instance, is preoccupied with issues of place and displacement, Edward Barker's poems eventually return to the commonalities of grounded experience, taking circuitous routes to get there, privileging the disruptive power of the word. Katy Evans-Bush can tell an offbeat story the way you've never heard it before, but wanted to. Her ironised yet romantic fatalism – reminiscent of a post-sisterhood Millay – is a model of edgy wit and restrained emotion. Heather Holden is some kind of forensic scientist of the recent past. Her gloriously mordant sensibility is at first a shock then a dark fascination. Simon Rees-Roberts' defence against the chaotic describes and comments on a landscape which, although mundane and suburban, carries an incipient threat as it is reinvented as exotic and internalised. Liane Strauss is wry and ardent by turns. These are tough-talking love poems that throw arms long and small around the Elizabethans and Coleridge. The resultant conversations rehearse the myth of the true-blue American moll.

All in all, this anthology will take you to many destinations unthought - of. It is sure to delight the poets' many fans, and surprise and charm many new readers.

John Stammers

This book is dedicated to Michael Donaghy

The pillar perished is whereto I leant,
The strongest stay of mine unquiet mind;
The like of it no man again can find,
From east to west still seeking though he went.
— Thomas Wyatt

Karen Annesen

Every dark place

Cast iron pans hung from hooks
over a formica counter and below that a place of miracles
where a gluey mass became a risen loaf.
Nearby the wood-burning stove was fed and stirred.
The logs must be laid like this, Father would say
and Mother would nod agreement and do it her way.
The light pine shelves lined with tins of peas
and green beans, boxes of cornflakes and bags of flour.

One day my sister stood on tiptoe, reached for a glass
and felt instead her hand on chocolate bars.
She searched for further secrets in every dark place
finding a rat who died for the love of cheese
and rows of old jam jars stuffed full of Mother's stories,
half-finished, wet with time.

Fair promises

Whatever I asked, she answered in proverbs.
She swept hard at the steps and didn't look up
when the men drove hounds
through town to the hunt. She said,
Not in war nor in peace
will a dead bee gather honey,
and I did not know what it meant,
but knew it was true.
After he hit me, again, she said,
Fair promises will make a fool happy,
then baked enough Welsh cakes
for a month of cold nights.
One day the doctor came
too late.
I told him,
Tomorrow is a stranger.

Telling the story

They met skipping
stones across a swollen lake.

A small breeze teased the afternoon.
She watched his wrist twist and his body

bend into the throw, her pulse
moving in rhythm with the stones.

Years later when telling the story
she skipped over that part,

hastened to the way his bright eyes flashed
as he picked up the biggest rock

then lobbed it into the water
laughing at the way it made her jump.

In the bedroom

The only colour in the room—
a vase the blue a baby's eyes might be.
What prepares you for such longing?

Mornings she searches the garden
for new growth. Today late summer
Michaelmas daisies tease with their lilac flowers.

Lilac is a healing colour
and she is not ready, yet.
There will be years still of this whiteness

which is not white, but an absence
of heat. Afternoons she paces
through all the rooms,

strains the hues from walls
painted in brighter times,
leaving a faint and bitter chill.

Waverly Station

The train does not want to leave,
protests with a slow chugging.

Can this be over?
It almost didn't begin.

The honeysuckle wasn't in bloom
as we'd expected. Who could have known

there would be such a determined grey?
The air tastes of singed hair: that split

second that cannot be relived.
You shout out the window: "Write,"

and we smile, our hands already
in our pockets fingering for words:

sometimes even the fastest train
doesn't take you where you need to go,

or switched tracks, sorry
for any turbulence, or goodbye.

Dinas Terrace

When you're lost in Aberystwyth on Christmas Eve
and the light is sliding, you might ask directions of anyone,
even the man coming out of his home with a saucepan.
He doesn't know, says, *Dinas means fortress in Welsh*.

His one front tooth juts toward you and a feather of white hair
floats on a wind that tastes of snow. You are nearly at the edge,
almost as far west as you can go. How lost can you be?
A woman drives by in a rusted truck smiling widely to herself.

In bed, later, you lay thinking of the man, the woman, the saucepan
and when you dream she proclaims her truck to be a fortress—
but you are humming some tune only just remembered.
Words tilt on the tip of your tongue.

Don't be mad

It could end like this: soft wind and rain on your face.
Or not. Tom's dad dead at 52 from too much of too much.
How do we know when to stop, much less how?

No way to choose the end. But if you could?
Surely music, fragrant violin or a crashing of piano keys.
People weeping of course, lots of them and mostly men
lacerating their hearts with memories of you golden.

You'd never end it alone and old, drunk
again, in a bar, some mid-west town late at night, saying:
Don't be mad, Mister, I just wanted to touch your face.

River mouth

Meet me where the Leithen
joins the Tweed.
Bring enough to sustain us
this long hot afternoon:
a blanket from the Mill shop, oatcakes,
apples (show me again how to eat them whole),
butter, ham and the stories you have yet to tell.

Leave the camera at home—
there are days that won't be captured
that way. And if we cannot hold
it in our minds then we don't deserve
such soft air,
this unexpected heat of May,
a stretch of river to ourselves.

Meet me under the tree,
I'll take your burdens from you,
the blanket, food and paper
and those thoughts not left behind
the ones about tomorrow and next year.
Meet me at Innerleithen.
Touch this river mouth with a kiss.

Filling Mia

We are filling you up
spooning in a view of the sea,
a moment bouncing on a
green garden chair,
being tossed up
against a big blue Norfolk sky.

Open your mouth,
let us fill you
with a walk along the quay,
fifty sailboats tipping their sails,
crabs in a bucket,
cakes by the beach at the caravan café.

There are hungers coming.
These days will always be there
jumbled together—
crabs and skies and sails,
and I will not.

How to fall

Easy, I've been doing it all my life.
On cobblestone streets
in high heels, yes.
Off a bike at seven,
your friend shouting faster,
some fear mixing in your blood
with yellow cake and pink icing.
Try a slapstick fall—
the ones where bodies
seem without bones,
seem to give way
somewhere low down.
Practice falling while smiling—
not wondering about your teeth,
the position of the furniture,
brain damage.
Off a train, out of a speeding car
like a stunt artist.
Remember to look like someone else,
like someone who doesn't fall for a living.
Then, when those moving trains no longer scare you,
try falling out of love
because you have to
with the one person
in whose eyes the world seems steady.
Or falling from grace,
not gently, but with alacrity,
get louder when told to calm down or shut up,
refuse to fall out of love,
laugh in public libraries.

Blakeney, Norfolk

Standing here beside the estuary
watching the tides go out
I should be watching you
but I'm thinking again of all I'll say
one day—oh, about men perhaps—
the way I first noticed their hands,
how their hands always give them away.

Or how, despite everything, they're worth it.
Maybe, if you catch me off guard on a warm night
like tonight—the first blue sky in a week—
I might be more specific, name names.
I'll tell you one day, say at sixteen
(that was a good year) not to be afraid to choose—
indecision is only a fear of death.

Choose a place, but travel often.
Choose a man early, but not the one
you think you can't live without.
He'll leave you babbling to yourself
midnight in a town with no cinema.
One day you'll see I've told you not to live my life
and what will that tell you?

The dunes

If you stay in that house you'll fossilise.
Get the purple bike, pedal fast
towards the honeysuckle path.
Then rest here a moment—tease
the golden centres out and taste—
no wine will ever match that clear liquid.

Look into the window at John's. He's not there.
Carry on alone (best get used to it)
and stop again by the grey pier where
water laps the rowing boats.
If you don't get in now you'll always
regret such hesitancy.

The smell of ice cream and sunscreen
is thick now and seagulls call overhead.
The pavement is half-covered in sand.
Pass the street where Loni will steal flowers
and blame you, pass the boys diving off the bridge
(soon they'll shout words you won't understand).

Ease your body into the shallow water
that high tide lets into the dunes.
The sun is on your back.
Beach grass bends in a breeze.
Below you your handprints appear and disappear,
appear and disappear in wet sand.

Edward Barker

That willow in seed
Huntergathering
Panoramic from the lights at the end of the runway
Early dawn
Soyuz
Rapt
Underground
Leadbelly's outdoor planetarium
The rain after rain
Absence
Gothenburg
Ghosting, just

That willow in seed

It's raining instructions out there,
it's raining tree-growing, fluff-spreading algorithms
that willow in seed:
dripping hieroglyphs, rosetta texts,
enigma codes whose rhythms drum
with the language of prayer before prayer
was the language of trees.

And as its seeds fall
with the codex of leaves it is even
spattering orchestral scores
each quaver packed tight
in a notation that bees can't read
but carry, Hermes-like, caught
in tufts of hair as they hover aloft
to be played later
by the next generation of leaves
                    way way downriver.

Huntergathering

Furred, the ur-man nurses a flame to life,
skillets a limp salmon, ferries it to the fire.
Fur-tongued, I rope a plosive,
corral the recalcitrant vowels
onto the plaza whose white parchment
blends tincture of titanium and garbage.
Both processes leave bones and charred remains
of dubious use to future archeologists.

Panoramic from the lights at the end of the runway

England; eggshell blue waiting rooms
where the lilac mother stares at her trainers, forgetting to wipe the
        baby's nose.
This is the twenty-first century, but we still have bats
and tears in the darkness of cathedrals
where the sweaty columns echo with the footsteps of tourists,

and April's cut another notch in her beaded belt
cause her Giro's lost in a Glasgow sorting house
and she hangs out on the wall with Warrior and the others
keeping score of the smokes and his lidded hood.
England of the summer's lilac clouds
so poised in their floating, bouyed and tethered
in the skies above Heathrow, trying to avoid the path of the jumbos
grazing the heavens while they hold the hands of the big leafed trees,

and down the road the van's come
to the chippy's back trap to offload
a month full of fat to recycle into what —
bisquits and soap? Morgan's wheelchair,
with racing tyres sloping inwards
so he can take the corners faster
is going to arrive today, and his fingers twitch
round the strap of his day-glo helmet,
while the stadiums are silent and their bars deserted
so Fuzzy's going to try it again on the midweek lottery

before hitting the betting screens with his mate and the Howler
though his eyes are streaming with excema and his shoes
have been rotting since Easter. England miasmic, England
diaspora of souls.

Early dawn

Odd, but a Neanderthal's head
has appeared in the folds of the duvet.
I don't mean like Coppola's horse
with its gore and blood, but like
a child's cloud, the face
or rather the side of his head
has just formed by itself
with the thick ledge under the eye socket,
the drawn down eyebrow, the gaunt
bulge in the cheek, and he looks
so much like me as he stares
not up at the ceiling
but about 40,000 years into the future,
my ancestor, his gaze stern,
the wisdom that comes from suffering and struggle
silently pleading with me
not to fuck it all up.

Soyuz

He's pedalling in his little metal box,
listening to Enya on a tape.
He can see the world out the window,
all blues and greens, and the white spiralled atmospheres
clearer and more beautiful than anything on earth,
like watching a child take
her first steps. The music fills him.
He misses people.
He feels like the last man
not on earth.

If he doesn't pedal, his bones will shrink
ten percent a month, his muscles
will waste away. So he's pedalling for his life.
There is no post, no junk mail.
His mom won't call, to remind him to
wrap up warm. There's condensation
in the capsule. It's tiny too —
you get stir crazy.

He's bicycling and bicycling and bicycling,
on and on and on, not getting anywhere at all,
and Enya sings her lullabies in his ear
but the world revolves under him
as he bicycles round it every twenty minutes
and sometimes it feels like there's an
invisible chain from his bike to the world
and he's making it turn with all the pedalling.

The earth is all alone with its
beautiful seas and its lightning
that makes the clouds glow
like a disco far away and he remembers
the people walking
coming and going over the cobbles of the big square
and the GUM department store —
and if he pedals they'll keep on walking
and with Enya in his ear he can keep on pedalling.

Rapt

Burnished, that slab of peach-coloured sky
rusting visibly as it hangs
under the gunmetal of a cloud,
ten thirty at night; the afterglow of our star.
In the vault above the bacon'y streaks of leftover evening
there's an astronaut blue going on
which has beaten off those sodium streetlights
who lorded it over nightwinter.

The air is sniffing round the tree-roots
and round the fat green leaves.
They lay their placid hands over the streets
making you feel intimate
with the night
like this magnolia's own blossom
is really just a promise
that we will find love
                that we already have.

Underground

Nobody's speaking, except for Bruised Nails
who gets on with a small brown paper bag;
'Excuse me, but I'm homeless' and
we all switch off, — plus
a white-bearded hippy

who boards later, braided ponytail
but his laces done sharply, sharply.
O God, are we still talking
or is this just interference?
Now everybody's reading

pot-noodle novels, the results,
the way we can't look at each other,
a horizontal elevator with our lives
flickering past, the wheels sparking shadows

way down the tunnel,
conduits snaking . . . where? why?

where we the shy ones will get counselling later.

Leadbelly's outdoor planetarium

Mine's a cummerbund
yours is a crowd —
his is a beagle
hers is endowed.

Ours is the night
in mosaical form;
quadrants of Lapis,
Orion, the dorm

of the Pleiades
embossed on the prow,
mine's a squeeze
of Europa, loud

exeunting, pursued…
you know what I mean:
pillowcase, lavender bag, a lewd
evangelist in a dishdash

rants to the cars
on the overhead
while underneath
they dance to Prince
in quince.

The rain after rain

The rain after rain's been raining
trips up over itself:
a stuttering, liquid orchestra of spatters,
light, almost soundless spoks
that fall onto moist black earth,
while harder, shrill tintinaments
drop from the gutter into a baked clay plate.

And you, shy, hesitant ones
lingering on the black bough, unwilling
to let go, fall, among the rooftops irregular staccato,
do you remember your days
of high cumulus? Do you listen
for that smallest of the olive leaf's vibrations
in the stillness of the afternoon
that will unseat you,
you and your saddled id?

Absence

Snow on the road. The drifts like waves
high on the banks have filled the verge
and spilled over. A line of beech, and one of firs,
their branches sagging with the weight.
One of them breaks and echoes like
a gunshot muffled far away.
Silence returns. A windless white.
There by that patch of darker ground
where wind has blown the newer snow
off frozen moss and wisps of stubble,
a nest has fallen to the floor.
The light crust's broken through to powder
there where the paws have left their bowls
in an erratic hieroglyph, weaving.
No blood.

Gothenburg

The tincture of distilled elk-musk
rises from the *Universitäte* labs late evening
and drifts towards the jagged triptych formation of stratus:
silverback, eglantine, streaked with coal-dust.

And the slope of a bridge arcing high into rivermist
whose far end disappears into the rainbow
of its fluvial histories;
here the escutcheon of the East India Company,

there the spice warehouse that paid
for the Stalinist palace of arts —
and silence too, lying on the waters,
snared in the ripples of a distant foghorn.

Ghosting, just

I will walk through the rain
and my neck will get longer,
more heron-like, for you.
Like a flamingo pinkens
as it threads the sulphur-thick waters
of the Serantibo,
I will bathe for you,
and as the shedding maple
feels constricted
by the city's pavement slabs,
I will grow leaves and be patient for you —
or crab-walk with an extra appendage
through the streets below the flickerings
of a dying sky to carry your groceries,
and I will bid you be happy,
be heron, be crab and flamingo,
as the world turns in its thoughts
and is intimate with you.

Katy Evans-Bush

Life (a dream) *Scene: the forest*
The bog of despair
The only reader
As the sun sends the sequins on my handbag scattering
Here
Cosi fan Tutte
Our passion
A later letter on art
The Metropolitan Opera
The escape artists

Life (a dream)
Scene: the forest

The room was small and the window was big.
The trees outside brushed green and yellow
on the clear panes and, but for the leaves, no sound
except for a little spaniel.
Bark! Bark! Bark! he remarked, into the glass-silence.

The air blowing in the window was also green.
Then Goldilocks had a dream in which she woke
and saw three bears
standing round her little bed,
gazing down at her with their eyes full of love.

And then an aeroplane puttered over the forest,
round and plump as a picknicking family
with a bag of cakes.

Mama Bear sighed and reached for Baby Bear.
Baby Bear was swelled with joy and Goldilocks
stirred a little but slept on
in the snug bed.
One hand curled round the edge of the counterpane
which was like a leaf.

Fondly the bears watched the sleeping pink child
and her curls, the colour of sunshine, fanned out
neatly on the pillow.
Baby Bear's pillow.

The people in the areoplane looked out
and saw the bears and saw the sleeping girl
and saw her wake and smile
and say to Baby Bear, What's small is big,
and heard her say, *Your room's a window.*

The bog of despair

We'd lunched on Greek salad and coffee
In a place with white walls and a skylight,
And when the guy in the corner's phone
Went off in a polyphonic can-can
We laughed without even trying to hide it.

We'd looked in a shop where a scarf
Of silk sat waiting for me to buy it,
And walked past a dog in a puddle
Of mud, who shook his coat,
But missed us — and we laughed.

The Heath was lovely that day —
The air was full of spring.
We'd walked up a foresty path,
Past a rubber hung like a thief on a tree,
Full of swag, and we'd laughed and laughed.

We'd walked past the swimming pond
And up the mound of Parliament Hill,
Talking about John Keats,
And other people we know, and the dog,
Looking for somewhere to sit, and laughing.

But every bench we came to
Was engraved in memory of someone
Loved and regretted, young, a child.
I imagined them sitting there
Along the hill, or invisibly playing.

The benches sat on a fat slope
Far from the blue chiffon horizon,
The blink of Canary Wharf,
The London Eye's diamond necklace.
We read them, and flinched, and laughed.

We turned and started down:
You had to get your kids from school,
And I had a shiny scarf to get,
And the jeweller's-window view
Of London had ceased to amuse us.

Your new shoes from Paris stuck
In the mud, and we laughed: the Bog
Of Despair! We laughed because
We could feel, behind us, up the hill,
The children watching us.

The only reader

As the book can only fall into temporary hands,
its spine cracked where one page or another's been favoured
by a boy in love with love or a homesick old man
till its glue dries up and its stitches disintegrate,
its leaves falling brown and acidic on someone's floor,
lines scattered randomly and perhaps thrown on a fire;

as the Canada goose honks serenely, unaware
of foreign towns below him (as only the sky
has meaning and tone) where foreign people gaze
through open doors at his leaf-and-cloud-coloured flight,
at the Amherst woods carried with him as he goes,
and the air momentarily clearer where he was;

as the curator loves the careful strokes of the scribe
but can know nothing of the man himself, who lived
a thousand years back, knowing only that he was a man
temporal like us and who lived for the oblique,
giving the gold-leaf ascender everything he had
because there was no other place to offer it;

so we keep dim faith with our craft; so the reader
pulls in illumination, and I send out my letter:
Dear Being, which art the Emperor of the Empirical,
and hope some electrical current will pick it up
to fly on a lightning-bolt like a rag on a kite-tail
so high on the hill that not even time can reach it,
and there's only the poem itself, and a goose going by.

As the sun sends the sequins on my handbag scattering

a train clacks over a stone bridge.
Inside it, my head's on your chest.
You look, and your hand stops moving;
you look up, your eyes bright, and say:
Ah, the lovely Calder! See its currents.
Beneath its grey water the fish swim out, uncaught,
their blue-green resplendence
in curious hidden turns.
As you talk of carboniferous limestone beds
you're dotted with gold specks thrown
by the sun, by my bag.
The bridge flashes past behind us;
banks of azalea wink and are tossed aside.
There was a stab, hard to see
if you so much as blinked, light on water,
perhaps a fin. Who knows what we're beginning.
I feel your muscles flex, and you lean
towards me again.

Here

I hold on to the knee-length grass, lowering
one foot and then the other down the chalky path
behind you in my split-toed Japanese-style
city trainers. You're in desert boots, talking.
You pull all the seeds from a stalk with one rapid
tug, laughing, and throw them over your shoulder.
The path cuts through the downs like a jet trail
dropped from the enormous mineral sky.

You tell me: *there's even a kind of beetle that only lives
here, a species of its own — the Whitehawk
variant something-or-other.* When I ask:
how do they know there isn't a family the same
somewhere in Nepal? You say there just isn't:
this place is unique. You ask if I'm okay there,
and I am. Anyway, you're used to rolling rat-arsed
down this hill, then waking next morning bruised,
bed-full of pollen, picking straw from your clothes
after too many pints of cider. Far down
a girl in the playground runs like a droplet.

A giant wood-louse; two snails, a narrow miss,
me slip-footed on the twisty surface.
They're lucky, you say, *I'd have had them for bait
another day!* But they're sedate as a WI lady
and her husband. I move aside and there
another Mr and Mrs emerge from the grass,
northwards, their necks craning gracefully out
under neatly-packed shells, pulsing lightly
with each quarter-inch they cover. Brave little snails,
slightly speckled, like no others anywhere.

Cosi fan Tutte

It was a summer night just made for singing.
The lights along St John's Hill were strung like beads
on a necklace, and I limped halfway
up to the late-night shop to get more wine
before I remembered my crutch, my still
half-broken bone springing slightly with each step.
My song, *fra gli amplessi*, seemed appropriate
to the scene unfolding now in your sweaty kitchen,
foretold two centuries before — a duet,
in pochi istanti, with some staying power
(you liked to brag that you had staying power,
but I don't think that was really the kind you meant).
Your nanny was right, the relationship was pathetic.
I'd left you both to fight it out below,
drunk, fighting over me; she thought as much,
Thought it was simple, thought she had the right,
her mascara streaked and you ponderously smoking,
darling, you're a bit common you know, admit it.
A bus went up the hill, weightless and bright;
Like me it had been up that hill before,
But this time the advert strung along it said:
ADMIT IT. YOU'VE BEEN HAVING AN AFFAIR.
Giungero del fido amante. What an adventure!
And now this. I could taste the air that night,
the blue-black so refreshing on the naked skin
of my left foot. Somewhere I heard a radio,
a different world. A sudden restaurant light
and a couple drinking under a pleated shade,
hands raised around thin stems, her bracelet gold
in the peach glow as she looked out at me.

Our eyes met and the moment froze. The crystal
set — I mean the set-up — I mean glass coffin –
lurched, and out popped my particular poison.
She looked away and I went on, awake.
the breeze cool after your kitchen, the corner shop
strangely the same. *Sconosciuta*, I think
I talked some nonsense, and I bought the wine.
He handed me my change. It didn't show,
a lui divanti. It was only me.
I turned and started down, still really walking,
in quest'abito verro, by myself,
not missing my gunmetal-grey support,
instead held steady by the net of lights.
Oh che gioia, I have to admit I sort of
got into it. But then, I also knew
from the bathos that you loved me. She didn't get it,
battering herself against a man,
il suo bel core, who simply didn't care.
No, of course she did, and she also got,
provera, her revenge, *nel ravissami!*
later on by proving to be pregnant.
Well, that was how it went — but as I told her
when she rang me up next day, still crying,
darling, you know, it's just what people do.

Our passion

The doe her buck, the bitch her dog, the cow
a bull or two to pull in earthly favour,

each girl a boy, each crone some wizened geezer:
it's like for like, each skin for same skin chosen.

And when the thing's done, what falls in between?
When neither cow nor bitch nor girl nor crone,

when likeness' likeness isn't for the choosing,
earth still exacts a choice, requires its flesh.

But look here: underneath the carapace
of skin, in each its own condition, kissing,

torchlight lights our red-cloaked silhouettes
of bone, capillary and empty space;

and what you see is not a choice, but living:
the ghost locked in its fellow-ghost's embrace.

A later letter on art

…and the artists I met were so technique I could not
stomach them. I was happy enough
washing dishes, establishing slowly my iron rule
over the kitchen at Timothy's on Zion St.
(I once sent you a picture, in which I wore
a yellow shirt and held a dishrag, remember?),
playing with colour and texture and building
an understanding of what is relative
or subjective, by living as an artwork.
Spending a life with one person — being one
when you are two — is that not a sublimely evocative
construct? Is that not art?
You wanted to feed me. Oh, let's not even go there,
just let me have a kiss to taste for the next couple of years.

The Metropolitan Opera

Sometimes, like on a 3D ruler where the disciples
eat, look around, eat, it's there
the way it always has been, its red-&-olive drab
plaid laid out with the perspective
of a medievalist, along the wall.
On it the father lies
with head to double-doorway and stockinged feet
to window, elongated like the couch, arms folded
in saintly repose.

The room looks paler in retrospect
than in fact it was, as if it were a fresco
on crumbling plaster, while around the house
echo voices whose names are spoken
with reverence, but not till after: Sills, Callas
(tragic non-sequitur in this age of faith),
Fischer-Dieskau. It's a play of light
that brings it up, the wintry glow
of 3pm on couchback, on the rough
upholstery's red-&-gold check, thin curtains hanging sheer
against the assaulted glass and outside's
secular grey-&-white; or else a strain of Verdi,
Puccini (who cried like a child in his room
when Mimi died by his own pen), Bizet,
where the honest peasant choir
leads us along till suddenly the beloved
breaks free and soars like a bird above the others,
her voice swirling tempestuously around the house,
and romance smashes in and becomes
the cathedral and everything it touches turns to gold.

The escape artists

Houdini never told. You asked and asked,
convinced there was some secret. And yet
when he came dripping out of that glass box,
a pile of broken chains on the floor by his feet,
was it not death he'd bit his thumb at?
How you all cheered. You were reborn en masse
in the power-surge of what he'd demonstrated.

But hadn't you spent whole afternoons
helping your children tie up handkerchiefs,
remove jokers, hammer false bottoms —
later looking down, or sideways rather
than at their familiar baby hands only half-concealing
full-sized coins? Ignoring rabbits
poking out of hats, and visible strings?
And what about the tin of sardines
brought from behind an ear? Wasn't that you,
mendacious conjurer? Wasn't that magic?

You don't need a tour of the whale,
its pink sitting rooms and corridors drizzling with damp,
to show you someone lived there
and what they made of it. You've seen the sword
in the umbrella stand, furled, incognito.
And that metallic plate hanging over your fireplace:
wasn't that once a dragon's scale?

Heather Holden

Voyeuse
A pair 1. *Silly buckets*, 2. *Blurry skies*
To the Greek who put me into the picture
Mistletoe
As I waited at *East Seven-Thousand*
Little ghosts of the industrial 1830s
Oubliette, Lancs
A cockling sea
To Weldon Kees

Voyeuse

Laocoön, I worry
every time I think of you,
escape-attempt realist.
Sometimes, Larry, I feel like you.

Houdini, I'm elated
when I think of you,
escape-attempt illusionist.
I feel like you, Harry, sometimes.

You both hold my attention.
Will you, or won't you, escape?

I am a goddess, who has spoken.
I am a goddess, who is uncertain.

A pair

1. *Silly buckets*

A cover girl's head's getting covered by a bucket,
vetch, ragged robin, herb robert, harebells, onto a magazine.

Holes in the top of a mop-bucket: being arranged,
wild flowers: one follows one's *Woman's Own*.

In an icy outside lavatory she douses herself, naked,
with buckets, to bring herself to salvation.

'She was always first up to collect mops and buckets
to wash the prison floors in the mornings.'

She said she stuck her head in a bucket and drunk all the blood.
She said it were like having a drink.

I went round with a petition for her.
I'd a few buckets of water threw at me. And flour. Said she.

Outside it buckets down, her on couch and him on chair
dozing, television-volume loud, much later.

2. *Blurry skies*

Churchyard, overcast fast-moving clouds.
Radclyffe Hall's sense deserts her
as religion clouds her desire.
The lips fester beneath a grey cloud of hair.
The sun breaks through. Reporters take note.

They are puffing clouds and giggling.
They're posing before 'photographers' storm-clouds'
(I quote Katherine Mansfield)
backdrops for moment-preservation.
Rosebay willowherb pours forth seed in clouds.

Recently-tarmacked road, stone pavements,
houses, roofs, moors, clouds. Murder. Why not?

To the Greek who put me into the picture

after Fray Hortensio Félix Paravicino y Artega

El Greco, it is most astounding —
you mirror more than retinal-factual,
your brush-tip pierces the actual
yet you depict a normal human being.

I look up from these holy books
to watch you as you do this painting —
the sun flashes red flames
along silk a spider is weaving, —
rays mustered from their bodies
trace diagrams they both must be hearing.

I reflect on him within your picture.
I leave him, here within your picture,
my soul, your soul, painted into your picture —
ut pictura, poesis. Amen.

Mistletoe

There is no escape into a fine, safe, unambiguous truth-discourse.

Rukmini Bhaya Nair

1.
As starflowers by black stone — my legs,
through grass — not cut, stroked —
over walls — not grazed — fluent,
as harebells are resilient to winds.

Rushes might prick, bog holes lurch,
sulk, blacken my socks,
snap my ankles in their puzzled surfaces
but cotton grass, galaxies, further

over the tops
to where a dioaxine-violet shadow
like an haute couture wrap
traverses the junior cloakroom, to where

amethyst-to-taupe shimmering brocade,
orchid organza with beaded copper leaves
and sky-blue faille come
to constitute my costume.

2.

He is already dark in the yard.
He is in the washroom entrance.
His whisper is *I'm here.*
He takes one arm to draw her
within one washroom.
You have the mistletoe?
You will use it?
He curves in to discover the mouth.

Her eyes move round dead steady
hair to spectacles
skylight, moonlight
initials, love-hearts on whitewash.

3.

There's a light on in the warm cave
and shelved brownpaper-packed books,
racks of boxes, of pencils, straws.

He locks the portal, leans back.
He beckons. Summoned, she goes over.
Light-switch to position OFF.

He undoes the neck of the female shirt,
then the next button, and the one following.
His hand gets a footing up the skirt.

He flicks the light-switch back to ON,
fastens up all the buttons,
picks up two boxes of Sweetheart straws,

he chooses two boxes the straw which sweethearts suck,
picks up two boxes sweetheart suckers,
unlocks the door, deports her.

4.
A blancmange-mould-shaped car,
pride of the driveways normally,
parked on a path to a disused quarry,
has steamed-up windows.
Inside, kissing is in progress.
The hand is up the skirt.
She regards condensation upon the windows.
It matches the paintwork, pearl gray.
Are you looking at something?
No. I always keep my eyes open.
Rustles sound from his pocket.
Perhaps he will be giving her a present?
He stops the kissing, takes her hand.
She feels warm liquid upon her hand.
He wipes her hand with his handkerchief,
starts the car and off they go
in the Standard Avant-Garde Phase II
and apart from lavender-orange mauve lenticulars,
world is wanton drizzle.

As I waited at *East Seven-Thousand*,

my message before arriving at this place had been
'And don't forget, my message is *resistant*,
a sycamore-twirl type Freudian slip, if ever,
an Ali-Nile-Ali mode of seed-dispersal.
I have nothing', I would have said,
'to say' — until I swore love-words,
in true promise of some place wholly past,
in foolish hope, as hope is surely comforting.

She was tidying her bed. I saw her blankets,
like my Greek brown one and cellular duck-egg blue one
bought in Whiteleys, way back whenever.
She'd been here alone in *Flatland* 'a while' she said.
She said to me, 'Be aware of me, adore me,
you are dear to me, this I promise. Do not grieve.'

Little ghosts of the industrial 1830s

There used to be a factory in Languedoc,
in Languedoc, where spiders were reared.
Their webs were woven into gloves and stockings.
Spiders must be kept in isolated pens,
for they fight, may even eat each other,
are very active and need a great deal of room.
There used to be a little factory in Languedoc.
In Languedoc, it was. It failed. The expense.

Their web is used for cross-hairs in instruments.
A man, by name of Rolt, with a little engine,
won a silver medal for winding off,
from the Royal Society of Arts, in London,
two miles per hour, from twenty-four spiders . . .
of cobweb, of cobweb, of cobweb.

Oubliette, Lancs

Our door was locked.
The coal hole had a loose plate
pig iron, square, with a pattern
a way back down, back in
in my school uniform, satchel first,
quick worm's-eye view up the street,
blackness, cat piss, a little coal.

My frame is a one-time cellar
I magnify to ten by three by seven,
white-washed millstone grit walls.
Let me get out of here, quickly
two L shapes, up a level, back
to the coal hole the following summer,
chasing our Sherri down the chute.
My parameters for this passage are
chute, coal, stench, ex-workbench
rusty pliers, wires, screws
study, lair, den, atelier,
laboratory, cats' lavatory.

I tried abstract expressionism down there
but too few foot candles
too dank for the masterpiece to dry.
I stood on grass on top of it, a tourist,
donkeys' years later, some time back now.

A cockling sea

'God,' said I, 'be my help and stay secure;
I'll think of the Leech-gatherer on the lonely moor!'

William Wordsworth

The news is Nineteen Cocklepickers Drown.
Some get, and some don't get, unlucky breaks.
I swim through stuff like this all night, head down.

I see you flying round like eider's down.
The tide was soon above the workers' necks.
The news is Nineteen Cocklepickers Drown.

You say that next day you'll be out of town.
It's not that far from Morecambe to the Lakes.
I swim through stuff like this all night, head down.

Upon the moor, how words got overblown
like leeches made those time-and-tide mistakes.
The news is Nineteen Cocklepickers Drown.

The best bit was the bit I wish we'd known.
A way was underway, not too complex.
I swim through stuff like this all night, head down.

Upon the lonely moor, you were my eidolon.
The sea-beast's gone. Now on the prom, joss sticks.
I swim through stuff like this all night, head down.
The news is Nineteen Cocklepickers Drown.

To Weldon Kees

Ketty Lester sang at your memorial and I saw her
singing *Love Letters* live at Rawtenstall Astoria,
seven years on.
It's a thread that connects us.

I felt shy standing right in front of her.
She was one foot higher, up on the stage.
Everyone else was slow dancing.
Weren't there others staring?
She looked in a bad mood
but you *can* look stern when concentrating.

Ketty Lester was and I knew her song.
So I concentrated on concentrating
on her concentrating on
love letters straight from your heart.

Simon Rees-Roberts

Aperitif

Everyone's happy as the picture-postcard
of the overweight, gnarled granny
who smokes a pipe and churns a hurdy-gurdy.
The shop next door sells varnished walking sticks
and pots of the inevitable jam
with little gingham lids. There's a rail
of T-shirts and backless cotton dresses:
fading, where the sun has crept around
a dark blue canvas awning. Afternoon
and white, injection-moulded café chairs
swelter on the overheated cobbles.
The old man with the clogs adjusts his cap
and lets the brake off on his donkey cart.
The children in the back start looking worried,
even here in this land of happy peasants,
where no one's left who can remember when
— at the inauguration of Rue Jean Moulin —
someone heard a creaking shutter close
and scanned the crowd to check who wasn't there;
or earlier, when priests were guillotined,
or when cartwheels growled under the weight
of bodies of the pustulated dead,
or when the only sound of iron on stone
was when the butcher's knives were being ground
and a granite saint looked down, as usual,
at some burgher being disembowelled,
on this spot, where I contemplate my drink.
Encore un Ricard, s'il vous plait, Madame.

News from another Surrey

I thought *business opportunity*:
small Espresso stall, donuts maybe,
something that would be… innovative,
but no one ever feels the need to eat.
It's been afternoon since I arrived,
I can't remember when — a while ago.
It's quaint: a lane with overarching trees,
like the one we saw when we got lost
going to your auntie's place in Guildford.
The flowers here are mostly red and white:
lupins, peonies, foxgloves, hollyhocks.
                    The blessed are resting on a grassy knoll,
primping up their floaty Swan Lake dresses.
Some seem as if they're always on the point
of getting airborne. Sometimes billowing
bits of chiffon drift into the breeze.
One of them has got a harp of course
— elevator music, you would call it.
A river flows… to make the waterfalls
look good, but I suspect that out of sight,
it's pumped back up, like at a Garden Centre.
                    The children here are all called Cherubim.
They lie about and grin. They're overweight
and don't take exercise, but no one does.
No one eats, or drinks, or sleeps, or that —
and women here are really quite attractive.
But sex is out, we mustn't think of it.
The last time that I looked I could have sworn
my genitals dissolved in heavenly light.
I'll stop now, but I could go on and on.

Mappa mundi

Tired of powering the South-East Trades,
a Zephyr in the corner of the page
pauses for a sharp intake of breath
and sucks in everything: Americas,
oceans, continents and *Here be Monsters*,
to the sound of parchment crackling around us.
Inside the wind it's raining tiny frogs
on cars gone belly-up, trashed trailer parks,
a bloated cow snagged on a fallen branch.
I pinch myself and find it's real enough
then start to rake back through the scattered junk.

I'm on the lookout for a party trick…
that galleon's sail could be a handkerchief,
unfurled to hide the swanky Rolex watch
a conjurer is hammering to bits;
but as I wait for our collective gasp,
he passes me a clutch of springs and cogs.
Wake up! Horizons tighten like a noose
and all that's possible is shrinking fast.
Watch the Great Ouroboros eat his arse.

Overheard

'Love you,' she said and something in her intonation
— the way her phrase had finished on an up —
implied a question, but she snapped her mobile shut
before she had a chance to hear, 'me too'.
Hell, what do I know? Not my conversation...
but the incident reminded me of you:
those times that you've demanded my attention
and I've withheld it. What else can one do?
The usual, pretend it isn't true
that repetition ratchets up the tension
manifest as silent eloquence.
I overheard you, sighing in the bathroom
and knew that 'sorry' wouldn't lift the gloom
and 'love you' wouldn't yet make perfect sense.

All the days drift

Although something lost usually clings for ages,
seems no reason's given; no help from trusted
psychoanalytic interpretations.
       Now I remember…

New Orleans cemeteries: our guide said that
when they opened a tomb, months later
(not sure why), well there was nothing except
       bones and cockroaches.

Where there's doubt it's wise to be anchored somewhere
concrete; something trivial yet exquisite:
snatch of half-heard hymn on a dud radio,
       thrown as a lifeline.

Envy faith: take St. Expedite's congregation
knowing prayers generate hardcash, vehicles
white goods, life everlasting and new lovers;
       simple equation.

All the days drift, pausing to rest at arm's length,
scrutinised by a cool presbyopic science.
Just accept what's known to be there and certain:
       there'll be an ending.

The emperor on philosophy

Last week at the observatory I watched
        my ancestors, the stars, consumed by fire.
I thought: perhaps their essence is returned
        through light and ash to nourish us somehow —
to fertilise as dung for sesame.
        Thus, part of my grandfather (bless his name)
might well become the leaf of some base plant
        which I might eat and, through it, be informed.
My new astronomer was not impressed
        and chided me, his views more orthodox.
He picked up some dividers, those they use
        to plot celestial movement and position.
Abstractly, he toyed with the device,
        splaying its legs and closing them again,
testing the sharp edge on his callused palm.
        The one may move away to slice an arc
as great and fast as any swallow can,
        but in the end comes back to meet the start
— that singularity where two were one.

So tighten the girths, adjust the snaffle bits,
        flush my fallow deer out of the wood
and watch their eyes dim as the arrows come;
        life is just a canter to extinction…
I could have waited — fought it out, at least
        become skewered meat on some sharp implement;
but no, this is the best course I can take.
        A greater enemy has joined the siege,
the river undermines the city walls;
        the cellars of our palace have collapsed.

What use is a delay? To close my eyes
          and summon several favoured concubines,
then try to recognise each by her scent?
          An excess of excess; I cannot find
a simple pleasure to excite the nerves.
          I have chased after novelty, not passion
and lost that edge on which I used to rock
          this way and that, towards a little death.
I have been troubled recently, I find
          that at that moment which we term sublime,
when pleasure, like a peony, bursts the bud
          and fills the veins with sherbet (so it seems)
that, strangely, I have not been really there.
          I find myself distracted, focussed on
the detail of some gilded ornament,
          a tassel or the pattern of a rug;
surely a sign that things have run their course?
          My bay mare, she's the first, my champion
bred of five generations of the best.
          There! Nothing for my enemy to harness.
Now my pretties. I know that my eunuchs
          would pass them on to any rude plainsman
who could spur their flanks to a gallop.
          My Circassian! Through the hashish smoke
her doe-eyes melt. Softly she speaks of love
          in the gurgling language of hot springs.
Place her by my side, so I shall feel
          her warmth — the high-tide ooze of ripples lapping
into the gunnels of my affection.

Now, one by one, the rest; that second point
which my astronomers record so well.
 The dagger does its work, the circle's closed.
No poison, I'll have none of that. A basin.
 Look, your emperor, shall cut his wrists.
And you, my friend, before it is your time,
 be kind enough to fetch some kindling.
Yes, fire! Where is your sense of urgency?
 We'll give them nothing, no hierarchy
of generals, lords, young catamites or slaves
 but leave them something less familiar
to feed their avaricious eyes upon
 — a dry, cold, grey democracy of ash.

The white

And I remembered staring at a screen
and typing any words to spoil the white
and wondering, why am I doing this?

Then if some words made sense or if a line
described the play of light across your cheek
I'd tie them fast around my floating wrist

to save me from the emptiness ahead
where I could never write another word
— attempt to render your familiar face.

I tried the negative, said snow is black:
the blizzard deadened sound, the world went dark
and all the galaxies still steamed apart

until we reached the point where stars go out
and Ursa Major and Andromeda
retained some vague, remembered afterlife

before we had forgotten names of stars,
the stars themselves and which way up is north
and marvelled that we had another breath.

I wish you were

The weather vane on the barn's gable
is flirting with the vagaries of breeze,
not like the reliable profile of a cockerel
who pans the compass from St Aignant's steeple:
analogue of the depression due.

Strange to think that this fey red admiral
who suns himself on a garden table
has a giant Amazonian cousin
whose original, languid flap of a wing
has started it, half a world away.

I found your postcard from New York,
the one I had been using as a bookmark,
blown into a border of verbena
and still damp from last night's shower.
Slugs, who like a diet of printed matter,
had chewed their way across downtown Manhattan.

With eyes closed the world becomes familiar:
I'm reassured it's not just work on paper.
The jet, miles up, and trucks on the by-pass
intrude less than the cicada's rasp;
but dead leaves stirred in the thicket,
over by the abandoned tractor
and no thrumming wings as accompaniment,
could be adder, lizard or axe-man.

The atmosphere so thick it's ploughable;
a sudden gust and the butterfly
is caught in a downdraft and is stuck
to the surface of the chlorinated pool.
Six legs flailing at nothing
as I contemplate whether to save him.
Instead, I turn over your card to decipher
from smudged ink, the message I half-remember,
forged from glowing thought before the Earth
was just hot air and flat:
            I wish you were…

Liane Strauss

Hymn
How to do things with words
Coup de foudre
Pointless
Muse
The yellow dress
Schweinehund
The name of love
Leaving Eden

Hymn

after Sappho

Immortal Aphrodite, though in your eyes
neither mercy nor the hunger of desire
can be detected, since they lie in your head
like the impress of a leaf in snow,
at full tilt you are riding here now,
the wings of your sparrows in my ears beating,
my heart demented and refusing to heed me.
I can see you will not be deterred.

So I implore you, Dread Goddess,
since you turn your cold ear to my tormented lips,
inspire me to your likeness in marble
that no one can see through me
and never, never in a thousand years guess
at the conversations that keep running with him in my head.

How to do things with words

Darling, would you mind terribly?
Scrambled eggs appeared before him,
the then-boyfriend,
and without uncoupling his eyes
from the morning whore text
(Knicks in Seattle? *The Zen of Investing?*)
he thanked me.
That was the first time I noticed
how you could do things with words.

Tone is everything.
The request sweetened with possibility
is command from woman to man,
with conspiracy, from woman to woman,
with admiration, man to woman,
necessity, man to man.
You can have pretty much anything
so long as you know who you're dealing with.
Words do the rest.
They really do have a life of their own.
I take up any old words at hand,
piece a thought together —
It's what I'm thinking.
If I stop to pick and choose them,
words become *Ideas*, even better.
A good one's like a German engine:
it can take me anywhere
and I can go years without retooling.

But the stars and crescent moons of feeling,
now that's magic.
Like the sorcerer's apprentice,
I simply utter a spell, "I love him," say,
under my breath or out loud in my head,
and my colour rises, my palms go sweaty.
Try it some time. Or substitute some other feeling
you never suspected and watch the buckets overfill,
the brooms sprout arms and legs and march and multiply.

The truth is, everyone does things with words,
whether or not they know it.
Consciousness is like an apple,
if it happens to land and you're Newton,
or even if like William Tell it's forced on you,
it changes everything.
Never again will you toss off a casual remark,
hazard an innocent question.
Things you've been saying for years suddenly sound stilted,
nonsense profound, meaning ridiculous.
You have to give up what's true along with what isn't
and just be grateful for fiction.
Nothing's real until you say it, and even then —
Knowing how to do things with words can be terrible.

As for the speaker who doesn't know that he's an actor,
it's an old story. Boy says, "Eggcup, I'm dying —"
and pauses for effect. Too slow! Too careless!
A kiss, a brandy, that's all he was after.
Instead, with the unshakeable conviction of a Stanislavski graduate —

Coup de foudre
peu après Laforgue

When the bolt struck I did not rush to the window
to see the bystander's hair unmanned,
the Galapagos of upturned umbrellas,
the avenue's implacable black buckle,
river and rise, rowboats at rooflines,
the eggs of inspiration agape against
the broken-winged bindings of consummation,
the apocalypse sprung full-blown from the word.
When the blind light came out of that nowhere
like an original thought, startling and unlikely,
shaken from the sky like foreign money
into the grass among the table crumbs
I sat here unreading the same sentence
in which I stumbled on the letters of your name.

Pointless

When you leave the room, though it seems empty
and cold suddenly, the way it can, the weather
notwithstanding, and so pointless I
wind down like a mechanical clock, every breath
another second slower, and everyone bores me,
most of all the ones with souls who sweat,
rubbing their two sticks so hard with no hope of fire
I can taste eternity, it isn't death.

When you show up I don't come alive
Coppelia-like, all six senses spluttering
like the kettle in the morning, shuddering
like a girl at the pictures at the scary part
and leap across the room in emulation of
my heart my heart my heart my heart my heart.

Muse

I'm the dame, and you're the dick.
My eyes are greener than the new kid —
Why does he look so damn familiar? —
My legs are longer than the San Andreas Fault,
and it's a call, but it's my heart
that's flawed and hard and colder still
than all the loveless bodies hard-knock cops
fish from the star-crossed, moon-lorn Bay
and blacker than La Brea's blackest pit.
That's how you see me.

And I can see that you're about to pour
that bleak long inextricable worn look
stiffer than the drink you just passed up
into the endless pitch of my impenetrable Ray Bans.
You're screening *Stairs of Sand* again.
The old print ticks with fraying static threads,
the murky script rises and surfaces
out of the soundtrack thick as blackstrap with cliché
like fresh rot from the dark
where I'm the con and you're the mark.
I'm the kiss and you're the tell.
You're the how, I'm the why.
I'm the blinding booze, the sucker bet,
and you're the loner with the heart of gold,
that fatal yen for just the kind of trouble you know better than to stick
your supersensitive neck out for and in spite of which,
because there's no such thing as love,
because no one ever does anything for nothing,
because you can't even begin to figure out what the hell you're doing here,
and I never asked you,
you won't stop until you save me.

The yellow dress

Inevitable city, coming back to you, like dreaming —
it all seems real,
I take for granted that it's half invented,
the headlong wind that brings on restlessness,
the bridge that vanishes halfway across the river.
Memories sleep and wake,
in between them I am drifting.
I know it's not that other summer's evening.
I recognize the past, it's nearer,
it's more vivid, the yellow dress
thrashing on the line
in the convent dormitory courtyard,
my Romanian roommate delirious with fever,
the day I skipped class
like there was nothing to prevent me
and we drove to the Camargue
to take in its 'unique and savage landscape',
according to you and your *Let's Go*,
the tall glasses of *pastis*,
the high late light, the chairs.
I slipped past but I took note,
you wanted to kiss me.
What followed after was unprecedented.

Schweinehund

These sour old men would swiftly trade ten years
for what we have in mind to do.
It's too hot in this corner
and we've been here for hours
but you somehow haven't noticed
that our promiscuous parley,
how far do I go, which way should I take it,
is starting bodily to try my patience.

You've brought me to The Dog and Duck,
surrounded me with hunting pictures,
and I appreciate the gesture.
But all those men with guns behave,
their dogs are too well trained.
I can't stop staring at that bird
hanging in rapture, a saint of Mannerism,
the S of her neck so lately rampant
all uncoiled, slaked, wrung,
eminent of every longing.

It's hard to breathe and hard to think
and I'm too coy and you're too charming
and then again my eyes keep straying
to where those wild old men taking their rouse
keep braying and drinking the long week's end, and how,
unblinkered and unblinking, they would trade a swift ten years,
and maybe more, maybe much more, while you keep talking
and my free hand in desperation goes to hold the hair up
off my neck but nothing helps.

This pub smells of dog, the doggy air is baying.
You're not shy but you're too literary
in this heat, and, in this heat, which comes at me
and comes at me, and at my back those keen old men —

I'm crushing out my cigarette.
I'm finishing my drink.
I'm licking my unliterary lips.

Tell me, my duck, how is it with you?
Tell me, what, exactly, are you going to do
when I let slip
this low-cut
high-heeled
fishnet
whore-hound
kiss?

The name of love

I don't care and someone else should see if they can suss
a name for tricks the past plays on the mind.
The inescapable grid after the game of chess.
Or when forgotten frozen scenes long dead
play back like ghostly answering machines
in a sudden power surge and bend the pulse
and break a sweat as if time had broken loose
and run back to dig up a buried thread.

As for the future scene that from that blue returns
ensorcelling the soul to heedlessly possess
the incandescent body of the present,
I propose the name of love, one more for the list
of words the clear-eyed Eskimo devised
for that which when you touch it melts and burns.

Leaving Eden

The motor's running and I'm leaving Eden.
It's gotten too small, too cramped, it's too green.
I've packed my bags, taken my best face cream,
shaken the apple tree until my wormy heart
fell at my feet.

It's not the serpent, I didn't need convincing.
It's not in my nature to be happy
to ignore what I know, can't remember
when I first went suspicious. If I'm
disenchanted with the past at least I'm something,
something to the core.

There never was a paradise on earth, a heaven.
Each fleshy fist of fruit harbours its seed.
Nothing has changed, nothing was ever
how it seemed in Eden, and if it was,
I can't imagine it was me.

The motor's running, the asphalt is seething,
my bare legs stick to vinyl slick with sweat.
The air of motion now will run
its fingers through me, and like Atlantis
underwater, I'll forget.